# Religious Studies (AS Ethics)

*Revision Guide for Edexcel*

*Foundation paper: Unit 1, Area B & Unit 2, Area C*

Peter Baron & Laura Mears

Published by Inducit Learning Ltd,

Mid Somer House, Southover, Wells,

Somerset BA5 1UH. United Kingdom

**www.pushmepress.com**

First published in 2014

ISBN: 978-1-909618-54-1

# Contents

# Acknowledgment

I am grateful to Henry Swales for permission to include in this guide original material from his revision summary sheets first developed for his students at Tonbridge School, Kent

# How to Get an A Grade

Effective learning involves reducing difficult topics into smaller, "bite-sized" chunks.

Every revision guide, card or study guide from PushMe Press comes with its own website consisting of summaries, handouts, games, model essays, revision notes and more. Each website community is supported by the best teachers in the country.

At the end of each chapter you will see an `i-pu-sh` web link that you can type into your web browser along with a QR code that can be scanned by our free App.

These links will give you immediate access to the additional resources you need to "Get an A Grade" by providing you with the relevant information needed.

Getting an A Grade has never been easier.

Download our FREE How to Get an A Grade in Ethics App for your phone or tablet and get up-to-date information that accompanies this book and the whole PushMe Press range.

http://ethics.pushmepress.com/download

# Introduction to Ethics

## NORMATIVE ETHICS

Asks the question "how should I act, morally speaking?" or "what ought I to do?" The AS "Religion and Morality" topic explores the connections between deistic spirituality and goodness.

A norm is a "value," meaning "something I think of as good." The normative theories we study at AS (Edexcel) are: Utilitarianism and Situation Ethics.

## META-ETHICS

Meta-ethics concerns the nature and meaning of ethics (what does it mean to say something is good?). It particularly focuses on ethical language. Meta-ethics is studied at **A2** level. A key meta-ethical question is:

> *"Is morality absolute - applying everywhere and for all time, or is it relative, specific to a time and place - a culture, situation or viewpoint?"*

## APPLIED ETHICS

Applies ethical theories to real world situations. The applied issues at AS (Edexcel) are:

- **WAR AND PEACE**

- **SEXUAL ETHICS**

However, the **UNIT 2** module provides an opportunity to examine a number of applied ethical issues, including Abortion, Euthanasia and Genetic Engineering, which are explored in the appendix.

## DEONTOLOGICAL

Acts are right or wrong in themselves (intrinsically) - it is not about consequences. Often stresses the rules or duties (Kant, Natural Law, Divine Command Theory). **DEON** is Greek for duty.

Although no individual deontological theory is studied at AS, it is important to be aware of a few of them, and what they stand for, so the merits and otherwise of teleological theories can be explored in an informed manner.

# TELEOLOGICAL

Teleological theories (telos = end in Greek) focuses on consequences of actions. An action is good only if it brings about beneficial consequences (it is instrumentally good, not intrinsically because actions are means to some other end like happiness or pleasure), for example, Utilitarianism and Situation ethics.

Four questions to ask of moral theories:

- **DERIVATION** - How does the moral theory derive (produce) the idea of goodness?

- **APPLICATION** - How can we apply the "good" to choices we make?

- **REALISM** - How realistic is the theory?

- **MOTIVATION** - Why should I be moral?

These questions will be answered for all moral theories in the final chapter.

## INTRINSIC GOOD

Something that is good in and of itself, and not by relation to some other thing. For example, telling the truth, even if it causes pain.

## INSTRUMENTAL GOOD

Something that is good in relation to its effects. For example, telling the truth because it pardons an innocent party accused of a crime, or more generally, serves the goals of justice.

# Religion & Morality

There has always been debate about the ways in which religion and morality relate to one another. The traditional view of the church is that morality is dependent on the existence of God as the grounding for moral values, or as the guarantee of divine justice. "The ways of the Lord are right; the righteous walk in them." (Hosea 14:9) One of the most well-known theories developed to account for this relationship is Divine Command Theory.

## DIVINE COMMAND - CHRISTIAN ABSOLUTISM

Morality depends on God's commands as revealed in Scripture. Sometimes called **THEOLOGICAL VOLUNTARISM,** Divine Command Theories are found in the Franciscan ethics developed by John Duns Scotus (1266-1308), William of Ockham (1285-1347), and Andrew of Neufchateau (1340-1400). Modern evangelicals take a similar view - see the **CHICAGO STATEMENT ON BIBLICAL INERRANCY** (1966) following Bible-based reformers Martin Luther (1483-1546) and John Calvin (1509-1564). A modern theorist is Philip Quinn. It is open to the problems of **EUTHYPHRO'S DILEMMA**.

## DEONTOLOGICAL

Something is good because God commands it and wrong because he forbids it - so creates duties (**DEON** = duty in Greek). In the Old Testament God is described as a commander of his people and lays down the law (Exodus 20:1-17). Disobedience is punished by death (eg Moses kills the worshippers of the **GOLDEN CALF**). God's **OMNISCIENT** and **OMNIBENEVOLENT** (all-loving) character underpins the law - gracious, compassionate, merciful, steadfast (Exodus 34:6). In the **NT** Jesus gives a new commandment to love (John 15:7) and says love entails obedience; "if you love me you will obey my commandments." So **AGAPE** is a divine command (if Jesus is God). **AQUINAS** argued that when Abraham went to slay Isaac he did no wrong because "the Lord of Life and Death commanded it, " (Genesis 22:1-2) and so Abraham would not have been guilty of murder.

## INITIAL PROBLEM

The problem of **ABHORRENT COMMANDS** occurs because, with Abraham and Isaac, God appears to approve of murder, and when the angel of the Lord commands Joshua to kill everyone in the cities of **JERICHO** and **AI**, Joshua is apparently not guilty of genocide (Joshua 8). God is also described as **JEALOUS** (Exodus 34:6-8) and will not tolerate rivals such as **BAAL**, the god of the people of Palestine. The 450 prophets of Baal are killed by **ELIJAH** after the challenge - who could rain down fire from heaven? (1 **KINGS** 18:33). Andrew of Neufchateau suggests Abraham would have sinned had he not gone to kill Isaac, even though Isaac was saved by the ram caught in a thicket. In the New Testament Jesus orders the demons to enter a herd of pigs that stampede into the sea (Mark 5), and commands storms to cease and illnesses to be cured: "Be clean!" exclaims Jesus to the Leper.

# EUTHYPHRO

**EUTHYPHRO'S DILEMMA** originates with **PLATO**. Is something good because God commands it, or does God command it because it is good? If goodness = God's commands, there is the **ARBITRARINESS** problem (we need to know God's reasoning too, and if there is no God presumably there is no morality either and "anything goes"); the **EMPTINESS** problem (that the statement becomes an empty **TAUTOLOGY**\* where "God is good" is the same as saying "God is God" which doesn't get us very far); and the **ABHORRENT COMMANDS** problem - that God appears to order genocide in the book of Joshua and practising gays to be stoned in Leviticus. In a **PLURALISTIC** society there are many views of God and what he is saying, and even if we take the Bible as **AUTHORITATIVE** divinely-inspired words, there is still the question - what do those words actually **MEAN**? Language is open-ended and must be understood in context (eg "do not kill" can't be an absolute because Joshua is ordered to slaughter the people of Jericho). So if God's commands are immoral, that makes God immoral - and if goodness comes from elsewhere, that makes God irrelevant to morality - and God himself should be condemned for ordering the **GENOCIDE** of the inhabitants of Jericho and Ai.

# CHARACTER

But Philip Quinn argues "the divine essence constrains the divine will." The essence of God is his essential **CHARACTER** - all-loving, all-knowing and all-powerful. We don't know everything and have to trust God's essential goodness eg in commanding Joshua, because we don't know what would have happened otherwise. So God's command to torture the innocent is conceivable, but impossible given God's character - he would have to be arbitrary and unloving. However on this basis we have to say **JOSHUA** was mistaken because God could not have possibly commanded genocide. Where does this leave the **AUTHORITY** of Scripture and God's supposed commands in Joshua 8?

## SOURCE OF MORALITY

There are only three possible sources of moral value: **DIVINE COMMAND**, **REASON** and **EXPERIENCE**. **REASON** implies either **KANT'S** a priori method (universalisability) or Aquinas' a posteriori method (looking at observable goods). Utilitarians argue for **EXPERIENCE** of consequences and their relation to general happiness - an empirical measurement - and **SITUATION ETHICS** argues that there are no rules, only **LOVE** and its relation to consequences. However we must recognise that **REASON** is not a neutral idea - different cultures reason in different ways (eg Buddhist philosophy is very different to Kant's). And if there is to be agreement in a **PLURALISTIC** society this can only come through supplying reasonable grounds for sharing a common value - such as the one Kant gave, "universalise your actions," and indeed Jesus echoes "do to others as you would have them do to you" - the **GOLDEN RULE** (Matthew 7:18). Moreover different cultures handle the **BIBLE** in different ways - **CREATIONISM** is much bigger in the US where court cases are still being fought over **EVOLUTION** vs six day creation, and most of us would argue it is not necessary for "women to keep silent in church" (1 Corinthians 11:13) and, anyway, in Acts 21:9 we read that Philip the evangelist had "four daughters who prophesied," so casting doubts over the view that no women held public leadership. How **ABSOLUTE** is any command?

A **TAUTOLOGY** is defined as a repetition of the same idea in different words: "God's commands are good because God commands them" becomes "God's commands are commanded by God."

# EVALUATION

In "Can man live without God?" modern Christian thinker Ravi Zacharias claims that without a moral law-giver, there can be no moral law, and everyone knows there are some things that are right and wrong. Public disgust at paedophilia, pointless animal cruelty and domestic violence may be a few serious examples. On a lighter note, Radio 2 runs a confessions slot where votes are taken from the presenter on whether the confessor should be forgiven. A man rang up and confessed to going to the supermarket to buy the Christmas vegetables on Christmas Eve to find not a sprout, carrot, or potato in sight - all was sold out. Panicking, he saw an old lady whose trolley was filled with her pre-ordered items, and when she was distracted, he ran to the check-out as quickly as he could. No one in the studio could find a redeeming feature for this confession - all unanimously declared it "wrong." Although there are grey areas in morality which differ from culture to culture, perhaps we subscribe to more absolutes than we admit, and if so, where do these come from if not from an ultimate, external authority?

Perhaps our discomfort with the account of the near-sacrifice of Isaac (Genesis: 22) is related to a misunderstanding of its significance. Throughout Jewish history, Yahweh God defined himself apart from all foreign gods by his abhorrence of child sacrifice: "Fathers should not be put to death for their children, nor children for their fathers; each is to die for his own sin." (Deuteronomy 24:16) Abraham's willingness to obey God against all reason showed his dedication to "love the Lord with all his heart, soul and strength" (Deut 6:5), a demand that Israel needs to grasp in order to see how offensive and abhorrent the worship and practices of false religions. Without an understanding of this, how can Israel begin to attempt to understand the destruction of Baal worshippers or the flood? God's provision of the ram caught in the bushes both confirmed his abhorrence of child sacrifice and pointed to

God's ultimate provision of a substitute once and for all, in his son Jesus. The abhorrent deed did not take place; God's character has not changed, but impressed upon Israel indelibly is the command to put God first, and the reassurance of his provision for sin.

## GET MORE HELP

Get more help with religion & mortality by using the links below:

http://i-pu.sh/F1R47K39

# Utilitarianism

## BENTHAM'S ACT UTILITARIANISM

**BENTHAM** (1748-1832) was a social reformer who believed that the law should serve human needs and welfare. He was writing during the **AGE OF ENLIGHTENMENT** - a time where, following the substitution of individualism for tradition, a number of believing and non-believing thinkers were trying to formulate a moral theory which took human nature, and the needs of the majority, into account. As a "non-theist," (a non-believer, who believed that no-one could be atheist, or say for certain that there was no God) Bentham looked for a maxim which encouraged moral behaviour, without relying on biblical or church teaching. In the writings of Frances **HUTCHESON** he found the phrase "greatest good for the greatest number," and this seemed particularly applicable at the time. In the inadequate housing and poor sanitation of town-life in **POST INDUSTRIAL REVOLUTION BRITAIN**, Bentham saw greedy factory owners capitalising on the ready supply of workers who had flooded in from the countryside. Without the often paternal protection of landowners, the working classes found themselves treated as disposable labour with few rights, having to rely on charity or face the workhouses if they could not work due to ill-health or death. For a more detailed picture, read the novels of Charles Dickens or watch the brilliant BBC mini-series "North and South" (or read the book by Elizabeth Gaskell) - you are required by the syllabus to have a good grasp of the social and cultural context for the theory.

Through the application of Bentham's theory, as well as the efforts of other social philanthropists, conditions improved, and Bentham's thinking can be seen in the **REFORM BILL** of 1832, the **FACTORY ACTS** of 1833 and 1847, as well as prison reforms and even the abolition of slavery.

Where **JUSTICE** was **RETRIBUTIVE** he wanted to see it **REFORMING** and acting as a **DETERRENCE** - there had to be a real social benefit outweighing the pain to the criminal, and with a better **DISTRIBUTION** of resources, but all in the cause of the **GREATEST HAPPINESS PRINCIPLE (GHP)** - the motive was to reduce suffering and increase happiness for everyone. The theory is **TELEOLOGICAL** because it measures likely consequences of **ACTIONS**, and **HEDONIC** because Bentham believed pleasure (Greek: hedon) was the key motive and could be quantified. So there is an **EMPIRICAL**, objective measure of goodness.

## Motivation

There is one **MORAL** good: pleasure; and one evil: pain. "Nature has placed mankind under two **SOVEREIGN** masters, pain and pleasure." Right actions are, on balance, pleasurable; wrong actions are, on balance, painful. Bentham's is therefore a theory of **PSYCHOLOGICAL HEDONISM** (hedonism - pleasure-seeking).

## Hedonic Calculus

The **HEDONIC CALCULUS** is a way of measuring pleasure and pain, so the consequences of an act can be assessed as a score in units of happiness called **HEDONS** (plus for pleasure, minus for pain). The seven criteria are (acronym **PRRICED**): Purity, Richness, Remoteness, Intensity, Certainty, Extent, Duration. In this assessment "everyone is to count as one and no-one as more than one" (Bentham), so there is strict

**EQUALITY**.

## *Quantitive Pleasure*

Bentham believed "pushpin is as good as poetry" (pushpin - a pub game equivalent to playing a slot machine in today's terms). Pleasure is purely **QUANTITATIVE** so we can't award more hedons to listening to Mozart or painting a picture. Mill, who was saved from mental breakdown by **WORDSWORTH'S** poetry, really objected to this. According to Bentham, we can compare a small child's delight in a new toy with someone else's delight in a new girlfriend. A **PIG** enjoying a good wallow is of more value than **SOCRATES** having a slightly sad think. Hence "the pig philosophy."

## *Pleasure Machines*

**JCC SMART** (1973:18-21) asks us to imagine a pleasure machine where we can be wired up every day and passively enjoy every pleasure imaginable (note - addiction often operates like this as a kind of refuge in a supposed pleasure - like drink). **ALDOUS HUXLEY** wrote of a brave new world where people popped **SOMA** tablets to make them happy (there were 41m antidepressant prescriptions last year in the UK). Bentham can have no problems with this, but **MILL** saw happiness as a wider idea involving **ACTIVITY**, and realistic goals and expectations (closer to what my therapist might advise or what **ARISTOTLE** argues).

## Strengths

1. There is a **SIMPLICITY** in Bentham's calculation and a radical **EQUALITY**.

2. The **TELOS** of increasing human welfare is attractive and **COMMON SENSE**.

3. His ideas drove **SOCIAL REFORM** and he designed a more humane prison called a **PANOPTICON**, never built in the UK, but in Barcelona.

4. There is a lack of snobbery in his classification of all pleasures as **EQUALLY VALID** - why should Mozart be thought better than Rap music (at least in giving pleasure)?

## Weaknesses

1. Bentham focuses only on **ACTIONS** so we have to keep on calculating (he doesn't allow us to have **RULES** to make life easier).

2. He equates **PLEASURE** with **HAPPINESS** - but they don't seem to be equivalent (ask the athlete training for the Olympics whether the toil is pleasurable - but it doesn't mean a lack of contentment with training).

3. We can always ask "you're going to the nightclub, but is that a **GOOD** idea?" ("Good" meaning "promoting your welfare"). Bentham implies pleasure is **MEASURABLE** (it isn't - how can we compare my hedon with yours?).

4. Finally, he has no answer for Smart's **PLEASURE MACHINE** or Huxley's **SOMA** tablet. Of course, they were writing two centuries later so even if his stuffed skeleton, residing in a

cupboard in London University, could talk, we don't know what it would say!

## Key Quotes

1. *"Nature has placed mankind under two sovereign masters, pain and pleasure. It is for them to point out what we ought to do as well as determine what we should do." Jeremy Bentham*

2. *"In every human breast, self-regarding interest is predominant over social interest; each person's own individual interest over the interests of all other persons taken together." Jeremy Bentham, Book of Fallacies, p 392.*

3. *"The community is a fictitious body," and it is but "the sum of the interests of the several members who compose it." Jeremy Bentham*

4. *"Prejudice apart, the game of pushpin is of equal value with the arts and sciences of music and poetry. If the game of pushpin furnishes more pleasure, it is more valuable than either." Jeremy Bentham*

# MILL'S RULE UTILITARIANISM

The weak **RULE UTILITARIANISM** (RU) of John Stuart Mill (1806-73) is a **TELEOLOGICAL** (telos = goal) theory based on a definition of goodness as the **BALANCE** of happiness over misery. This is a measurable, **EMPIRICAL** idea - measure the happiness effects of likely consequences - giving an **OBJECTIVE** measure of goodness. Mill was against the **INTUITIONISTS** which he found too **SUBJECTIVE**. Mill argues that happiness is most likely to be maximised by generally following a set of **RULES** which society has found, by experience, maximise utility. But the rules can develop and in cases of moral dilemmas, we should revert to being **ACT UTILITARIANS** (AU), or weak **RU** because the rules aren't absolute, but are **GUIDELINES**.

## Mill vs Bentham

Mill disliked three aspects of **BENTHAM'S** version:

1. The swinish implications of categorising all pleasures as of equal value -drinking beer vs listening to Mozart.

2. The emphasis on pleasure alone, as Mill was influenced by **ARISTOTLE'S** views on virtue (eg the importance of **SYMPATHY** for others).

3. The problem of **JUSTICE** and **RIGHTS** - how do we prevent one innocent person or group being sacrificed for the general happiness of the majority? So Mill devotes the last chapter of his essay to **JUSTICE**.

## Mill on Happiness

Mill's definition of a happy life has three elements: **PLEASURE** (varied and rich) and absence of pain; **AUTONOMY** (the free choice of a life goal); and **ACTIVITY** (motivated by virtues like sympathy eg Mill used to hand out leaflets advising about contraception and campaigned for women's rights).

"**HAPPINESS** is not a life of rapture, but moments of such, in an existence with few and transitory pains, many and various pleasures, with a decided predominance of the **ACTIVE** over the passive, and having as a foundation of the whole, not to expect more from life than it is capable of bestowing." JS Mill

## Higher and Lower Pleasures

Mill was saved from a nervous breakdown in his 20s by the **ROMANTIC MOVEMENT** eg Wordsworth's Lyrical Ballads. To him poetry was infinitely superior to **PUSHPIN**. So "better to be Socrates dissatisfied than a fool satisfied." The **LOWER** bodily pleasures (food, sex, drink, football) were of less value than the **HIGHER** pleasures (reading, thinking, listening to Mozart). So Mill followed **ARISTOTLE** in seeing education as of vital importance (the supreme Greek value is **CONTEMPLATION** to gain wisdom). Only a person who had experienced both could really judge the difference in **QUALITY** (so we say qualitative pleasure is superior to quantitative). He called those who hadn't experienced both "inferior beings." Does this make Mill a snob?

## Rules

Mill has been called an "inconsistent utilitarian" (Alasdair MacIntyre) because as his essay goes on he moves from **ACT** to **RULE** utilitarianism. We use generations of **PAST EXPERIENCE** to form rules, so we don't have to do a calculation to know whether **MURDER** or **THEFT** is "right." We inherit **BELIEFS** "and the beliefs which have thus come down are the **RULES** of morality for the multitude" (JS Mill). These are not fixed but "admit of continual improvement," so not **ABSOLUTE**. The **FIRST PRINCIPLE** is utility (or the Greatest Happiness Principle) and then **SECONDARY PRINCIPLES** (rules) come from this and are constantly evaluated against the first principle. Just as navigation is based on astronomy doesn't mean the sailor goes back to the stars every time - no, Mill reminds us, he uses an **ALMANAC** - so, argues Mill, human beings follow a code book of rules passed down from previous generations as the best way to be happy.

## Justice

Bernard **WILLIAMS** argued that Utilitarianism violates our **MORAL INTEGRITY** by encouraging us to do things we would find repulsive, like his example of Jim who is invited to kill one Indian as an honoured guest in order to save 19 others. This is the problem of **INJUSTICE** - the Southern States may have enjoyed lynching innocent people in the 1920s but this doesn't make it right. Mill argues that unhappiness is caused by selfishness, by people "acting only for themselves," and that for a person to be happy they need "to cultivate a fellow feeling with the collective interests of mankind" and "in the **GOLDEN RULE** of Jesus we find the whole ethics of utility" (JS Mill). So we need to defend personal **RIGHTS** and "Justice is a name for certain moral requirements, which, regarded collectively, stand higher in the scale of **SOCIAL UTILITY**, and are therefore of more paramount obligation, than any others," and "justice is a name for certain classes of **MORAL RULES**, which concern the essentials of human **WELL-BEING.**" Rights, justice and the virtue of sympathy stop selfish self-interest destroying the happiness of others. So we escape the problem of Jim and the Indians as we would never shoot one indian (violate their right to life) to save 19.

## Act or Rule?

**LOUIS POJMAN** argues (2006:111) that we can adopt a **MULTILEVEL** approach (this is what Mill seems to be doing in talking about **PRIMARY** and **SECONDARY** principles). So we can have three levels if we wish: rules of thumb to live by, which generally maximise utility; a second set of rules for resolving conflicts between these; and a third process - an **ACT** utilitarian one, for assessing a difficult situation according to the **GREATEST HAPPINESS PRINCIPLE** or GHP (eg lying to save a friend). But in this way philosophers like **JO URMSON** argue that **RULE** utilitarianism collapses into **ACT** utilitarianism. Mill might counter that we don't have the time, the wisdom or the resources to keep calculating every action and this multilevel approach is therefore **REALISTIC** and **PRACTICAL.**

## Strengths

**RATIONALITY** and **PRACTICALITY**. Utilitarian ethics rests on a rational calculation of numbers of people whose pleasure or happiness is maximised. There is a clarity and simplicity to this. **EQUALITY** is central. Bentham wrote "everyone is to count as one, and no-one as more than one." This radical idea implies that everyone has equal weight in the utility calculation. **MILL** adds equal **RIGHTS**. Suppose, on an equal vote, you all vote for my dismissal (or even death) in line with maximising general happiness? "The utilitarian emphasis on impartiality must be a part of any defensible moral theory." (Rachels, 2006:114). Finally, utilitarianism takes account of the **FUTURE** - issues of climate change, potential future wars and famines all suggest we need an ethical theory that takes into account those yet unborn.

## *Weaknesses*

**MOTIVE**: "Why should I maximise pleasure or happiness?" We can't agree how to define pleasure or happiness." Bentham and Mill don't notice the difficulty of the concept of "pleasure" a fatal objection at the outset," Anscombe (1958:2). Then there is a difficulty in making me think of the interests (happiness) of others. Mill tries to bring "sympathy" in as a kind of virtue or psychological motive. **DISTRIBUTION** problems emerge when I try to maximise **TOTAL** not **AVERAGE** happiness. For example, low tax for the rich may raise the total but reduce average happiness, because the 10% super rich are much, much happier. Finally **CONSEQUENCES** are hard to calculate if you don't have the omniscience of God. The **IRAQ WAR** may have seemed justifiable by the Greatest Happiness Principle - but looking with hindsight we might argue - better a Saddam Hussein in power than a million deaths?

## Key Quotes

1. *"It is better to be a human being dissatisfied than a pig satisfied; better Socrates dissatisfied than a fool satisfied."* JS Mill

2. *"Happiness is ... moments of rapture ... in an existence of few and transitory pains, many and various pleasures, with a predominance of the active over the passive ... not to expect more from life than it is capable of bestowing."* JS Mill

3. *"Whatever we adopt as the fundamental principle of Morality, we require subordinate principles to apply it by."* (Fundamental principle = happiness is good; subordinate principles = rules) JS Mill

4. *"By the improvement of education, the feeling of unity with our fellow-creatures shall be as deeply rooted in our character, and to our own consciousness as completely a part of our nature, as the horror of crime is in an ordinarily well brought up young person."* (= sympathy) JS Mill

5. *"To have a right then is, I conceive, to have something which society should defend me in possession of. If the objector asks why? I can give no other answer than general utility."* JS Mill

6. *"Justice is a name for certain moral requirements, which, regarded collectively, stand higher in the scale of social utility, and are therefore of more paramount obligation, than any others: though particular cases may occur in which some other social duty is so important as to overrule any one of the general maxims of justice. Thus to save a life it may not only be allowable, but a duty, to steal, or take by force, the necessary food or medicine, or to kidnap, or compel to officiate, the only qualified medical practitioner."* JS Mill

*(note - so RU collapses into AU)*

7.  *"I account the justice which is grounded on utility to be the chief part, and incomparably the most sacred and binding part, of all morality. Justice is a name for certain classes of moral rules, which concern the essentials of human well-being more nearly, and are therefore of more absolute obligation, than any other rules for the guidance of life." JS Mill*

8.  *Bernard Williams argues that "because our relation to the world is partly given by moral feelings, and by a sense of what we can or cannot "live with," to regard those feelings ... as happening outside one's moral self is to lose one's moral identity; to lose, in the most literal way, one's integrity." (Utilitarianism For and Against p104)*

## Confusions of Mill

1. Was Mill an Act or Rule Utilitarian? He is sometimes described as a **WEAK RULE UTILITARIAN**. Mill believed that generally we should follow the rule as this reflects society's view of what maximises happiness from past social experience. But when a pressing utilitarian need arises we should break the rule and so become an act utilitarian.

2. "Mill took Bentham's view that happiness equates to pleasure." Sometimes Mill seems to argue this, but it's truer to say Mill's view is close to **ARISTOTLE'S** that happiness means "personal and social flourishing." So to Mill the individual cannot be happy without the guarantee of certain rules and rights and clear goals to aim for.

# MODERN FORMS OF UTILITARIANISM

The syllabus mentions three modern versions of utilitarianism, and the best answers will include discussion and critique of at least one of them. Modern forms of Utilitarianism take into account the problems associated with using the word "happiness" or "pleasure" as the goal of decision-making.

## Preference Utilitarianism

Peter Singer is most clearly associated with this version of consequentialism, which takes into account people's preferences, which may or may not seek to maximise pleasure and avoid pain. Tyler and Reid (AS Religious Studies, Pearson, 2006) cite two examples: one of a marathon runner who exercises his personal preference to "run under conditions of great physical agony to achieve a personal best;" the other of a prisoner who would "rather face death than betray his comrades." In both examples, the preferred outcomes seem to elevate physical pain over pleasure.

The **STRENGTH** of this approach may be found in its **INDIVIDUALISM**. You only have to look at your own family to see that one person's desire to roll around in the mud on a Saturday afternoon with a bunch of broad-shouldered pals and an oddly shaped ball, may be someone else's idea of hell. Yet does Preference Utilitarianism **WEAKEN** the teleological nature of the argument? In the example above, the prisoner's preference may be considered for him a duty, and this steers very near to Kant's **DEONTOLOGY**, which places duty as the only good. In this case, it may be further argued that in the comparison of such a prisoner who prefers to be tortured and killed out of loyalty and a sense of duty, and one who prefers to give in quickly to the physical pain of a beating, there is an obvious moral distinction. Can these preferences really be given equal moral weighting? Is one preference not better than the other? If so, we are veering towards an absolutist (deontological) morality.

## Ideal Utilitarianism

GE Moore in Principia Ethica (1903) challenged the monistic definition of the good. That is, he believed that there was more to the good than just happiness; truth or **BEAUTY**, for example. Moore asks us to imagine two worlds, one full of disgusting ugliness and one full of things we consider beautiful. Even though the beauty is not causing happiness to anyone, or the ugly world causing pain, is there a clear answer to the question; which world is better? He concluded there was, and hence he believed that this thought experiment showed that beauty was an **INTRINSIC**, rather than an **INSTRUMENTAL** good. (See introduction for definitions of these terms). Therefore, according to his thinking, even if leaving a partner caused suffering to family and friends, a case could be made for it, if it yielded a beautiful result in terms of love and creativity.

A possible **WEAKNESS** of Moore's version of utilitarianism is the claim that beauty is subjective; what do these worlds look like? A pink bedroom scheme may look beautiful to my nine year-old niece, but her grandmother may choose to decorate her room very differently. Furthermore, how does the addition of beauty to the list of goods aid practical decision-making? Yet Moore's contribution may add **STRENGTH**. Utilitarians are often criticised for providing no grounds for arguing that telling the truth or keeping promises should be generally followed.  Yet pluralists like Moore can answer this criticism by saying that truth has intrinsic worth. Overall, perhaps Moore's greatest contribution to the utilitarian stable was to **BROADEN** the very narrow definition of desirable outcomes.

## Negative Utilitarianism

Also known as painism, this version was first put forward by Richard Ryder in 1990. In contrast to the above approaches, which broaden the definition of the good, negative utilitarianism seeks to avoid the problems associated with desiring happiness or pleasure, by **NARROWING** it further: the only good is that which seeks to **MINIMISE PAIN**. The **STRENGTH** of this approach is in its ability to discount sadistic or violent preferences, for example, in the case of ten guards gaining pleasure from beating a prisoner. Suffering is the only evil and no amount of pleasure can justify it. Yet as a **WEAKNESS**, is this approach **TOO NARROW**? Irenaeus argues that this world is a "vale of soul-making" (Hick's expression) and that suffering can bring reward, and should not be avoided. Discounting certain types of meaningless, brutal and severe types of pain and suffering, most people would acknowledge that there is a value to physical training, patient endurance, or breaking a bone to re-set it, for example.

## GET MORE HELP

Get more help with utilitarianism by using the links below:

http://i-pu.sh/Z0T84M57

# Situation Ethics

Situation Ethics is a **NORMATIVE** theory (tells you what is right/wrong - what you ought to do), that is **TELEOLOGICAL** and **CONSEQUENTIALIST** (acts are right or wrong if they bring about good/bad consequences, or can be seen as instrumentally good/bad) and **RELATIVIST** (there are no universal rules as actions depend on circumstances; there is just one general universal value - that of agape love). It is also **CHRISTIAN**, based on the principle of sacrificial love (**AGAPE**).

## *Introduction*

Joseph Fletcher (1966) argued there are three approaches to ethics:

1. **LEGALISTIC** - someone who follows absolute rules and laws. Fletcher rejects this as it leads to **UNTHINKING OBEDIENCE** and needs elaborate systems of exceptions and compromises.

2. **ANTINOMIAN** - (nomos is Greek for law, so anti-law) or someone who rejects all rules and laws (Fletcher rejects this as it would lead to social **CHAOS**).

3. **SITUATIONAL** - Fletcher argues that each individual situation is different and absolute rules are too demanding and restrictive. Instead we should decide what is the most **LOVING** course of action (**AGAPE**). The Situationist has respect for laws and tradition, but they are only guidelines to how to achieve this loving outcome, and thus they may be broken if the other course of action would result in more love.

However, Situation Ethics is not **FULLY** relativist: it has an absolute principle (love) that is non-negotiable.

## Four Working Principles

In Situation Ethics there are **FOUR WORKING PRINCIPLES** (Fletcher's own term)

1. **PRAGMATISM** - (what you propose must be practical - work in practice).

2. **RELATIVISM** - (there are no fixed, absolute rules - all decisions are relative to **AGAPE** love. If love demands that you steal food, then you should steal food.)

3. **POSITIVISM** - (Kant and Natural Law are based on reason as both theories argue reason can uncover the right course of action). Fletcher disagrees with this: you have to start with a **POSITIVE** choice or commitment - you need to want to do good. There is no rational answer to the question "why should I love?"

4. **PERSONALISM** - (people come first: you cannot sacrifice people to rules or laws)

## Six Fundamental Principles

1. Nothing is good in itself except **LOVE** (it is the only thing that is absolutely good, the only thing with intrinsic value).

2. Jesus replaced the law with love or **AGAPE** ("The ruling norm of Christian decision is love, nothing else." Joseph Fletcher).

3. Love and **JUSTICE** are the same thing (if love is put into practice it can only result in fair treatment and fair distribution).

4. Love desires the good of **OTHERS** (it does not have favourites, but this doesn't mean we have to LIKE them).

5. Only the **END JUSTIFIES THE MEANS** (if an action causes harm, it is wrong. If good comes of it, it is right).

6. Love's decisions are made in each **SITUATION**.

## Strengths

1. It takes **INDIVIDUALS** and their needs seriously.

2. It's **FLEXIBLE** and also allows us to make judgements in situations where two moral principles **CONFLICT**.

3. **LOVE** is an important value somewhat neglected by other theories as the sympathy of Mill's utilitarian ethics is not quite as strong as the **AGAPE** of Joseph Fletcher.

4. It is important to see Situation Ethics within its time; it was natural that the baby boomers wanted society to be better; not characterised by prejudice and aggression, perhaps even politics.

5. Bringing people of different beliefs, races and backgrounds together played its part in promoting **EQUALITY.**

## Weaknesses

1. **LOVE** is a very demanding value to place at the centre of your ethics - can anyone love sacrificially all the time? Mustn't we be selfish some of the time?

2. Like all **CONSEQUENTIALIST** theories it's impossible to calculate into the future making this particular love calculation **IMPOSSIBLE**. William Barclay argues that Fletcher fails to realise the value of law - as an expression of the collective wisdom of generations before us, so the moral law is a guide which we shouldn't throw away so easily.

3. Law also defines the **FABRIC** of society. The effect of JAT Robinson's book "Honest to God" was explosive and comprehensive in reaching all parts of private and social life via the Media. In her autobiography, Quite Contrary, "Clean Up Britain" campaigner Mary Whitehouse wrote: "Before 1963 was out I found myself having to help children whose personal lives had been directly and adversely affected by the licentiousness and immorality which increasingly characterised television programmes." Could part of the legacy of the free love licentiousness of situation ethics be the child sex scandals at the BBC, not to mention the spread of HIV/AIDS? If so, has the theory done more harm than good?

## Key Quotes

1. *"Love alone is always good and right in every situation."* Joseph Fletcher (1966:69)

2. *"There can be and often is a conflict between law and love."* Joseph Fletcher (1966:70)

3. *"Too much law means the obliteration of the individual; too much individualism means a weakening of the law ... there is a place for law as the encourager of morality."* William Barclay

4. *"Love is the ultimate law because it is the negation of law; it is absolute because it concerns everything concrete."* Paul Tillich

5. *In 1952 POPE PIUS XII called situation ethics "an individualistic and subjective appeal to the concrete circumstances of actions to justify decisions in opposition to the NATURAL LAW or God's revealed will.'*

## Confusions to Avoid

1. "Situation ethics is Christian relativism." This idea needs careful handling. In fact there is one non-negotiable absolute at the heart of Situation Ethics - agape love. But this is a principle, not a rule. Therefore as it is applied, it is made relative to the most loving outcome. Fletcher himself describes Situation Ethics as "relativistic" as it "relativises the absolute, it does not absolutise the relative." Compare Fletcher with Pastor Dietrich Bonhoeffer who believed the most loving thing was to join the 1944 Stauffenberg bomb plot against Hitler (an action which cost him his life).

2.  "Jesus was a situationist." Again, be careful about a bland statement to this effect. Jesus maintained he "came not to abolish the law, but to fulfil it," although a key part of his mission seemed to be to overthrow the old Jewish purity code (he didn't like stoning adulterers, see John 8, or treating unclean women as "impure and untouchable," see Mark 5, both required by Leviticus 18-19). The young man of Mark 7 is commended for keeping the law but then invited to "give up all his possessions and come, follow me!" The nearest Jesus comes to situationism is in the discussion of the parable of the Good Samaritan, where the teacher of the law is invited to "go and do likewise" in each situation requiring agape love (Luke 10:29-37). Indeed, the parable is worth studying in the light of Fletcher's teaching. It's about the meaning and application of agape love.

3.  "Situation Ethics and Utilitarianism are very similar." They have similarities; both reject deontological approaches. Yet they also have differences: Utilitarianism has many forms but Situation Ethics is relatively undeveloped in recent times. You may like to develop this comparison, as the syllabus welcomes such debate between theories.

4.  If you mention Bonhoeffer, be careful not to write of him as a supporter of Situation Ethics. He lived and died before its advent, and even if he had not been executed in 1945, it is doubtful whether he would have agreed with it, stressing as he did, the importance of personal piety.

## Evaluation

In "Can man live without God?" modern Christian thinker Ravi Zacharias claims that without a moral law-giver, there can be no moral law, and everyone knows there are some things that are right and wrong. Public disgust at paedophilia, pointless animal cruelty and domestic violence may be a few serious examples. On a lighter note, Radio 2 run a confessions slot where votes are taken from the presenter on whether the confessor should be forgiven. A man rang up and confessed to going to the supermarket to buy the Christmas vegetables on Christmas Eve to find not a sprout, carrot, or potato in sight - all was sold out. Panicking, he saw an old lady whose trolley was filled with her pre-ordered items, and when she was distracted, he took them and ran to the check-out as quickly as he could. No one in the studio could find a redeeming feature for this confession - all unanimously declared it "wrong." Although there are grey areas in morality which differ from culture to culture, perhaps we subscribe to more absolutes than we admit, and if so, where do these come from if not from an ultimate, external authority?

Perhaps our discomfort with the account of the near-sacrifice of Isaac is related to a misunderstanding of its significance. Throughout Jewish history, Yahweh God defined himself apart from all foreign gods by his abhorrence of child sacrifice, "Fathers should not be put to death for their children, nor children for their fathers; each is to die for his own sin" (Deuteronomy 24:16) Abraham's willingness to obey God against all reason showed his dedication to "love the Lord with all his heart, soul and strength" (Deut 6:5), a demand that Israel needs to grasp in order to see how offensive and abhorrent the worship and practices of false religions. Without an understanding of this how can Israel begin to attempt to understand the destruction of Baal worshippers, or the flood? God's provision of the ram caught in the bushes both confirmed his abhorrence of child sacrifice and pointed to God's ultimate provision of a substitute once and for all, in his son Jesus. The abhorrent deed did not take place; God's character has not changed, but impressed upon Israel indelibly is the command to put God first, and the reassurance of his provision for sin.

## GET MORE HELP

Get more help with situation ethics by using the links below:

http://i-pu.sh/H4P76P25

# War & Pacifism

## JUST WAR THEORY

**JUST WAR THEORY (JWT)** is an attempt to provide conditions for **WHEN** war is acceptable and rules for **HOW** war should be conducted. It has its roots in Roman philosophy (especially **CICERO**), but was developed further by Christian theologians like **AUGUSTINE** (354-430) and then later by **AQUINAS** (1225-1274). Early Christians were **PACIFISTS** (based on Jesus' teaching such as "love your enemies" **MATTHEW** 5:44), but this situation changed after Constantine converted to Christianity after the **BATTLE OF MILVIAN BRIDGE** in 312 AD (as the Roman empire needed to defend itself against the northern tribes). JWT has three parts **JUS AD BELLUM** (literally "right to war" in Latin, so the morality of going to war), **JUS IN BELLO** (literally "right in war"), the moral rules conditions for fighting wars, and more recently in the 20th century **JUS POST BELLUM** (right after war, or the moral rules for establishing a just peace after conflict).

# JUS AD BELLUM

**JUS AD BELLUM** describes six conditions for **WHEN** it is morally right to go to war.

1. **RIGHT AUTHORITY** - a state may only go to war if a decision is taken by an appropriate and legal authority.

2. **JUST CAUSE** - there must be a good reason for going to war = **INJUSTICE** = self-defence or defence of others, for example, UK treaty obligations to defend Poland in 1939.

3. **JUST INTENTION** - must go to war with the right intention or motive: Aquinas "to promote good and avoid evil."

**FRANCISCO SUAREZ** and **FRANCISCO DE VITTORIA** (16th and 17th Century) added three more:

4. **LAST RESORT** - force can only be used when all other means of resolving the conflict have failed, for example, diplomacy and sanctions - such as sanctions on Iran and Syria in 2011.

5. **REASONABLE CHANCE OF SUCCESS** - deaths that happen in a hopeless cause are not morally justifiable.

6. **PROPORTIONALITY** - the benefits of waging war must be proportionate to the expected evils and harms caused eg don't go to war over fishing rights.

## JUS IN BELLO

**JUS IN BELLO** sets out three rules on how to conduct war:

1. **PROPORTIONALITY** - the methods used by soldiers must be proportionate: they should not be excessive to the ends they are seeking. For example, don't use an atomic bomb to enforce a UN resolution.

2. **CIVILIANS** - should never be directly targeted as happened in the Second World War in the bombing of Coventry or Dresden.

3. **MILITARY NECESSITY** - using the minimum force necessary to defeat the enemy: all military action must be necessary.

## JUS POST BELLUM

Brian **OREND** (The Morality of War 2002) suggests the following principles:

1. **JUST CAUSE FOR TERMINATION** - A state may terminate a war if there has been a reasonable vindication of the rights that were violated in the first place, and if the aggressor is willing to negotiate the terms of surrender. These terms of surrender include a formal apology, compensations, war crimes trials and perhaps rehabilitation. Alternatively, a state may end a war if it becomes clear that any just goals of the war cannot be reached at all or cannot be reached without using excessive force.

2. **RIGHT INTENTION** - A state must only terminate a war under the conditions agreed upon in the above criteria. Revenge is not permitted. The victor state must also be willing to apply the

same level of investigation into any war crimes its armed forces may have committed.

3. **PUBLIC DECLARATION AND AUTHORITY** - the terms of peace must be made by a legitimate authority, and the terms must be accepted by a legitimate authority.

4. **DISCRIMINATION** - the victor state is to differentiate between political and military leaders, and combatants and civilians. Punitive measures are to be limited to those directly responsible for the conflict.

5. **PROPORTIONALITY** - any terms of surrender must be proportional to the rights that were initially violated. Draconian measures or any attempt at denying the surrendered country the right to participate in the world community are not permitted.

## Strengths

1. Sets out clear **MORAL GUIDELINES** for going to war.

2. Influences the **BEHAVIOUR** of soldiers and politicians who may be brought before the International War Crimes Tribunal at the Hague (for example, the Bosnian war leaders).

3. It is **REALISTIC** - war is sometimes necessary to save lives and protect the innocent.

4. It is **UNIVERSAL** - and the basis for the work of the **UNITED NATIONS** and the **GENEVA CONVENTION**.

## Weaknesses

1. The **PERCEPTION** of the justice of war depends on a relative perspective, for example, the **US WAR ON TERROR** after the terrorist attack of 2001 led to the setting up of **GUANTANAMO BAY** detention centre in Cuba to hold people without trial. But the detention centre is arguably an unjust way of treating people in a war that is ill-defined (as wars against terrorists have to be).

2. The conditions are **AMBIGUOUS**. All wars involve the death of civilians (strangely called **COLLATERAL DAMAGE**) as it may be impossible to distinguish between a soldier and civilian.

3. It is **INAPPROPRIATE** for an age of terrorism when the aggrieved peoples (eg Palestinians) have **NO STATE** and hence are excluded from the ethics of just war theory which requires a legitimate authority. Are brutal states like **SYRIA** really a just authority? Who decides?

4. Impossible to know the **CONSEQUENCES** and so we can only apply **JWT** looking backwards. Who would have agreed to the **IRAQ WAR** of 2003 had we known the level of casualties (mainly civilian - over one million Iraqis have died)?

# ABSOLUTE PACIFISM

**PACIFISTS** (Gandhi, Martin Luther King) argue violence is always wrong. It doesn't matter what the situation is. Violence should be met with a path of **PASSIVE RESISTANCE** (non-co-operation or even love of the enemy).

Reasons for absolute pacifism include:

1. **JESUS'** teaching to "love your enemies" and "turn the other cheek" (meaning "never retaliate") in the **SERMON ON THE MOUNT** (Matthew 5) is echoed by **PAUL** who wrote: "Do not take revenge but leave room for God's wrath" (Romans 12:19) and gave the injunction to "repay evil with good."

2. **QUAKERS** oppose war as they believe violence is destructive and builds a cycle of violence and revenge. The only way to break this cycle is the path of **AGAPE** love - to be prepared to sacrifice oneself for peace.

3. **CONSCIENTIOUS OBJECTORS** refuse to fight wars on grounds of conscience. One famous objector was Bertrand Russell, who was imprisoned in 1916 for opposition to the war. "Fear has invaded our inmost being," he wrote.

## Criticisms of Absolute Pacifism

1. Fails to acknowledge **HUMAN SINFULNESS**. Reinhold **NIEBUHR** argued for **CHRISTIAN REALISM**: we cannot achieve ethical ideals (such as pacifism) because sin is present in everyone (especially self-interest and the desire to control others). Christians must sometimes use force to fight evil and establish **JUSTICE**. In the context of rising **FASCISM** war is an evil but necessary to prevent evils.

2. Fails to protect the **INNOCENT**. Elizabeth **ANSCOMBE** argues pacifism is immoral as it fails to protect the innocent and those who may suffer genocide. It denies the right of **SELF-DEFENCE**.

3. Failure to act (**OMISSION**) is as morally blameworthy as acting. **SINGER** and the utilitarians argue that consequences define the goodness and badness of an act so if we fail to stop eg the genocide in Bosnia we are morally culpable.

## CONTINGENT PACIFISM

Jonathan Glover (Causing Death, Saving Lives) is a **UTILITARIAN** who cannot adopt an **ABSOLUTIST** position. He does argue for a cultural shift away from war and because war rarely generates good consequences justification for war will be **RARE**.

Augustine was also a **CONTINGENT PACIFIST**, arguing that we cannot use violence to defend ourselves (turn the other cheek). But this counsel of perfection cannot apply to others. We do have the duty to protect the innocent in acts of **SELF-SACRIFICE**.

# GET MORE HELP

Get more help with war & pacifism by using the links below:

http://i-pu.sh/M8F50J34

# Sexual Ethics

## ISSUES SURROUNDING SEXUAL ETHICS

What does it mean to be human? Is there one universal shared human nature?

Are gender equality and same sex attraction equally ethical issues?

What values give meaning to sexual relationships (such as fidelity, chastity, commitment - which seem to be changing)? Are the **VIRTUES** a better way of analysing this issue?

How have developments in understanding the biology and **PSYCHOLOGY** of the human person affected sexual ethics?

Sexual ethics thus shares concerns and insights from **PSYCHOLOGY**, **BIOLOGY**, and **SOCIOLOGY**. With the prevalence of pornography, sex trafficking and decline in old models of family life, there can be few more pressing ethical issues facing us. At **AS** we study four issues:

- **MARITAL** (the role of contraception and non-procreation within marriage)
- **NON-MARITAL**
- **EXTRA-MARITAL** (adultery)
- **HOMOSEXUALITY**
- **DIVORCE**

# SEX AND EVOLUTION

Homo Sapiens emerged around 150,000 years ago. As social life developed so a primitive **MORALITY** created rules and boundaries around sexual intercourse. Sex changes its function from **REPRODUCTION** to **SOCIAL REGULATION**.

Religions emerge that created **PURITY CODES**. These involved **TABOOS** (the declaration of certain practices as unclean). For example the purity code of the Hebrew Bible, **LEVITICUS**, lays down a code of uncleanness - which included **BLOOD, INCEST, ADULTERY**, and **SAME SEX RELATIONS**. These are abominations punishable by social exclusion or death.

Such attitudes are reflected in attitudes to **WOMEN**. Women came to be seen as **PROPERTY** of men. Virginity was prized. Up to 1872, married women in Britain had to surrender all property to their husbands; there was no concept of marital rape until 1991 and violence against married women was only outlawed in 1861. In 2011 there were 443 reported incidents of "honour crime" (violence, forced marriage and even murder) in the UK.

A concept of what is **NATURAL** emerged and with it psychological **GUILT** for those who did not conform. It's hard to believe that in 1899 **OSCAR WILDE** was jailed for two years hard labour for homosexual relationship. **HOMOSEXUAL SEX** was only legalised in 1967.

# KINSEY AND THE SEXUAL REVOLUTION

The Kinsey report of 1945 shocked America. Intimate surveys of real people's preferences revealed:

- 10% of men were homosexual for at least three years of their lives. How then could sexual preference be **UNCHANGING**, fixed and uniform?

- 26% of married women had extramarital experiences of different sorts.

- 90% of men masturbated.

- 50% of men had been unfaithful to their wives.

# CHRISTIAN VIEW OF SEX

## Natural Law

Aquinas taught that there were three rational ends of sex, arising from the **PRIMARY PRECEPT** of reproduction:

- To have children.

- To give **PLEASURE**.

- To bind husband and wife together.

His view - that sex was for pleasure, was widely condemned, Aquinas wrote "the exceeding pleasure experienced in sex does not destroy the balance of nature as long as it is in harmony with reason." Right reason involves a delicate balance of the three purposes of sex - and avoidance of irrational or animal extremes. So the following sexual sins were forbidden:

- **RAPE**

- **CASUAL SEX**

- **ADULTERY**

- **HOMOSEXUAL SEX**

- **MASTURBATION**

Aquinas' view echoed the erotic celebration of sexual ecstasy in the **SONG OF SONGS** in the Hebrew Bible where sex is a sacred gift and picture of a mystical union, and one of the highest spiritual as well as physical forms of being.

*Behold you are beautiful, my love;*

*behold you are beautiful;*

*your eyes are like doves,*

*Behold you are beautiful my beloved, truly lovely ...*

*Your two breasts are like two fawns,*

*twins of a gazelle that feed among the lilies ...*

*You have ravished my heart with a glance of your eyes .*

*(Song of Songs 1:15; 4:2, 5 & 9)*

This is one of two parallel strains in the Bible - one positive and one negative, and the positive strain, that sex is to be celebrated, is echoed by Jesus himself, quoting Genesis 2:24, "from the beginning God created them male and female, and for this reason a man shall leave his mother and father and be united with his wife, and the two shall become one flesh. So what God has joined together, let no-one divide." (Mark 10:6-9) See also Paul in Ephesians 5:31.

## *The Negative Strain*

There is also a negative strain in Christianity which sees sex as dangerous, unclean, and sexual pleasure as sinful.

**AUGUSTINE** wrote that marriage was the "first fellowship of humankind in this mortal life," and "good not just for producing children, but also because of the natural friendship between the sexes," although primarily "a remedy for weakness, and source of comfort." Ultimately the good of marriage lay in its "goodness, fidelity and unbreakable bond."

Augustine argued against the **PELAGIANS** who saw sexual pleasure as a **NATURAL GOOD**, evil only in excess. Augustine agreed with Paul that since the **FALL** the body had been subject to death, "our body weighs heavy on our soul" with its sinful desires. Augustine believed that since the fall desire had been tainted by **LUST**. So sexual pleasure in marriage needed to be moderated by reason.

Sexual desire ("the carnal appetite") outside marriage, and sexual activity that results, "is not good , but an evil that comes from original sin." This evil of carnal lust can invade even marriage - so it is **DANGEROUS** and needs to be treated wisely and carefully.

After the **FALL** (Genesis 3) men and women were "naked and ashamed." The man's member is "no longer obedient to a quiet and normal will." Humankind was in danger of running away with lust for each other.

**CONCLUSION**: Augustine argues that precisely because the body is created good, it can be used wrongly, and this goodness has been deeply stained by the Fall. Sexual desire has to be circumscribed by **MODESTY**, chastity and wisdom.

## CATHOLIC TEACHING TODAY

The Roman Catholic Church teaches that sex has two functions - procreative and **UNITIVE** (binding two people together). Procreation is primary. According to Humanae Vitae (1967) these two elements are **INSEPARABLE**.

> *"Sexuality becomes fully human when it is integrated into the relationship of one person to the other in lifelong gift of a man to a woman." Catechism 2338*

**CHASTITY** is the virtue of self-mastery (Catechism 2339). It is expressed in friendship towards our neighbour. Sex outside marriage is "gravely contrary to the dignity of persons and of human sexuality which is naturally ordered to the procreation of children." Catechism 2354

**HOMOSEXUAL ACTS** are "intrinsically disordered. They are contrary to the natural law. They close the sexual act to the gift of life. Under no circumstances can they be approved." Catechism 2358

**ADULTERY** is absolutely forbidden by the sixth commandment and Jesus' words.

**CONTRACEPTION** - in 1951 Pope Pius XII officially permitted the rhythm method, but otherwise Humanae Vitae (1967) upholds the view that anything that breaks the natural relationship between sex and conception is wrong.

## Evaluation of the Catholic View

Professor Peter Gomes of Harvard University argues that the Bible bans one **CULTURAL** expression of homosexuality - a  promiscuous one and "never contemplated a form of homosexuality in which loving and faithful persons sought to live out the implications of the gospel with as much fidelity as any heterosexual believer." The Good Book (1997)

The Catholic interpretation of natural law implies that the primary function of sex is reproduction. But suppose the primary purpose is **BONDING**, then the argument that sex is purely for reproduction falls down - we can be Natural Law theorists and disagree about the secondary precepts (which Aquinas always argues are relative).

The Catholic **ASSUMPTION** (following Aquinas) is of one human nature. But psychology suggests there are varieties of human nature (heterosexual, homosexual, bisexual) because of genes or environment.

The prohibition on **CONTRACEPTION** seems irrational in a world of overpopulation and **STDs**. If **PRESERVATION OF LIFE** conflicts with **REPRODUCTION**, surely preservation of life is the primary primary precept?

# SITUATION ETHICS - CHRISTIAN RELATIVISM

Joseph Fletcher sees his own theory as **RELATIVISTIC** (even though it retains one absolute principle, agape love) because any decision is made relative to circumstances.

**ABSOLUTE** rules must be rejected as authoritarian and unloving.

Biblical prescriptions should be followed as wise **ADVICE** but abandoned in extreme situations if love demands it.

Fletcher argues that many applications of morality are never discussed in the Bible: "Jesus said nothing about birth control, homosexuality, pre-marital intercourse, homosexuality, sex play, petting or courtship." (Fletcher, p80).

> "It seems impossible to see any sound reason for any of the attempts to legislate morality. It is doubtful whether love's cause is helped by any of the sex laws that try to dictate sexual practices for consenting adults." (Fletcher, p80)

**AGAPE** love (unconditional love) is the only norm. The situationist is not a "what asker," ("what sexual practice is allowed?") but a "who asker." It's about **PERSONALISM** - people come first.

## Evaluation of Christian Relativism

**AGAPE** is too high a standard for our personal relationships, usually governed by self-interest. Why should I be loving (rather than pleasure-seeking)?

The vulnerable (young, homeless, poor) need the protection of laws preventing **ABUSE** and **EXPLOITATION**.

We cannot predict **CONSEQUENCES** eg unwanted pregnancies or **STDs** happen to people not expecting them who may honestly believe they love the other person.


## HOMOSEXUAL ACTS - A TEST CASE

We have already seen that the Catholic Church condemns homosexual behaviour as intrinsically disordered because of the assumption of one **UNIFORM HUMAN NATURE**. The situationist takes the opposite view; such legalism is unloving and so wrong. Is there a middle way?

In the **ANGLICAN** church there are two gay bishops (in America) and many practising gay priests. **VIRTUE ETHICS** indicates there is a third way of analysing homosexual behaviour. Which **VIRTUES** are present in the relationship? The **EXCESS** of promiscuity is condemned, but faithfulness, care and compassion can apply in any relationship irrespective of orientation. By the same argument the **DEFICIENCY** of abstinence is also a character **VICE**.

The moral issue surrounding homosexuality should therefore be about the promiscuous lifestyle and irresponsible spread of disease (as with heterosexuals). The legalism of natural law or over-emphasis on the code of Leviticus blinds us to the true moral question. What **VALUES** do we need in order to **FLOURISH**?

## KANT on SEX

Kant asks us to commit to build the moral world - the **SUMMUM BONUM** or greatest good, by following the rational principle he calls the **CATEGORICAL IMPERATIVE**. This principle has to be applied in all similar circumstances without conditions - it is **ABSOLUTE**. We have to act in such a way that we can imagine a universal law where everyone follows the rule that is generated.

Humans have intrinsic **VALUE** as "ends in themselves." We must be given equal dignity and respect as autonomous rational beings.

We share an irrational nature of passions and instincts with **ANIMALS** but we can rise above these and order our lives by reason. Human sex will be different from animal urges.

**LUST** disturbs reason. By desiring someone simply as an object of pleasure (rather than seeing them as a whole person, with dignity and reason) we dishonour them and violate their special uniqueness as a free person. We sink to the level of animals.

> *"Sex exposes mankind to the danger of equality with the beasts ... by virtue of the nature of sexual desire a person who sexually desires another person objectifies that person ... and makes of the loved person an object of appetite. As soon as that appetite is satisfied one casts aside the person as one casts aside a lemon that has been sucked dry." Lectures on Ethics*

**MARRIAGE** is the best expression of our sexuality. The pleasure of sex is acceptable (ie not animal) because two people surrender their dignity to each other and permit each other's bodies to be used for this purpose - it is a mutual **CONSENSUAL CONTRACT**. Reproduction is not the end of sex, Kant argues, but lifelong surrender to each other in a context of love and respect.

## Evaluation of Kant

Kant appears to separate our **ANIMAL** nature from our **RATIONAL**. This dualism explains why he still sees sex as something belonging to the animal nature. But **FEELINGS** and **REASON** cannot be separated this way, many would argue.

Kantian ethics produces **ABSOLUTES** (Categoricals). So the absolute "no sex before marriage" applies here. But in the modern era such absolutes seem to deny the possibility of a **TEMPORARY** committed relationship - or even sex for fun.

It's possible to be a Kantian and accept **HOMOSEXUAL MARRIAGE** but not **ADULTERY**.

## UTILITARIANISM

What do the utilitarians say about our four issues: contraception, pre-marital sex, adultery and homosexuality? Here we contrast **MILL** (1806-73) and **SINGER** (1946- ).

Mill is a **MULTILEVEL** utilitarian who follows a more **ARISTOTELEAN** idea of happiness - **EUDAIMONIA** or personal and social flourishing. He argues that we need **RULES** to protect justice and **RIGHTS**, which are the cumulative wisdom of society. But when happiness demands it, or a **CONFLICT** of values occurs, we revert to being an **ACT** utilitarian - hence multilevel (Act and Rule) utilitarianism.

Mill agreed that **CONTRACEPTION** was moral as it increased personal and social happiness, through family planning and restrictions on population growth. Today the British Humanist association writes "if contraception results in every child being a wanted child and in better, healthier lives for women, it must be a good thing." Mill was imprisoned in 1832 for distributing "diabolical handbills" advocating contraception.

Mill had found a murdered baby in a park. The practice of exposing unwanted children was widespread. Hospitals for **FOUNDLINGS** such as **CORAM** set up in Bristol in 1741, did little except institutionalise **INFANTICIDE** (child killing). Between 1728 and 1757 33% of babies born in foundling hospitals and workhouses died or were killed.

On **HOMOSEXUAL** rights Mill follows Bentham in arguing for "utilitarian equality" by which everyone's happiness counts equally. Bentham was the first philosopher to suggest legalised **SODOMY** in an unpublished paper in 1802. Freedom was a key to personal flourishing, and as long as no harm was done to any but consenting adults, it is a private matter how people order their sex lives.

In his essay on **LIBERTY** (1859) Mill argues for **SOCIAL RIGHTS** so we can undertake "experiments in living" that give us protection from the prejudices of popular culture and "the tyranny of prevailing opinion and feeling." Mill would have approved of **COHABITATION** and pre-marital sex.

## Evaluation of Mill

Mill was a father of the liberalism we take for granted where difference is tolerated. His brand of utilitarianism balances social justice and individual freedom and pursuit of happiness.

Utilitarianism works well looking **BACKWARDS**. The Abortion Act (1967), the Homosexual Reform Act (1967) and the Divorce Reform Act (1969) are all examples of utilitarian legislation.

Utilitarian ethics works less well looking forwards. We cannot predict

**CONSEQUENCES**. So the **AIDS** epidemic can be seen as a product partly of personal freedom to adopt a promiscuous "unsafe" lifestyle. It is hard to see how a utilitarian can prevent this or even argue it is wrong if freely chosen.

Many of the greatest **SOCIAL** reforms have not been inspired by Christian values, Natural Law or Kantian ethics, but by **UTILITARIAN** considerations of social **WELFARE**. Today relatively few Christian churches accept the complete equality of women.

## PREFERENCE UTILITARIANISM

Peter Singer defends the utilitarian line advanced by Mill and argued that with **HOMOSEXUALITY** "If a form of sexual activity brings satisfaction to those who take part in it, and harms no-one, what can be immoral about it?"

On **ADULTERY** preference utilitarians approve of any sexual activity which maximises the preferences of individuals, taking account the preferences of all those affected. So incest, bestiality, or adultery would all be acceptable.

Singer argues for **CONTRACEPTION** as population growth is one of the most pressing utilitarian issues, we should "help governments make contraception and sterilisation as widespread as possible" (Practical Ethics, page 183). But overseas aid should be made conditional on adoption of contraceptives.

## Key Quotes

1.  *"The only purpose for which power can be rightfully exercised over any member of a civilised community against his will, is to prevent harm to others. His own good, either physical or moral, is not sufficient warrant."* JS Mill

2.  *"If a form of sexual activity brings satisfaction to those who take part in it, and harms no-one, what can be immoral about it?"* Peter Singer

3.  *"The pleasure derived from the union between the sexes us a pleasure: therefore, leaving aside the evils, which derive from that source here is why the legislator must do whatever is in his power so that the quantity in society is as high as possible."* Jeremy Bentham

4.  *"Sex exposes mankind to the danger of equality with the beasts ... by virtue of the nature of sexual desire a person who sexually desires another person objectifies that person..and makes of the loved person an object of appetite. As soon as that appetite is satisfied one casts aside the person as one casts aside a lemon that has been sucked dry."* Kant

5.  *"It seems impossible to see any sound reason for any of the attempts to legislate morality. It is doubtful whether love's cause is helped by any of the sex laws that try to dictate sexual practices for consenting adults."* Joseph Fletcher

## GET MORE HELP

Get more help with sexual ethics by using the links below:

**http://i-pu.sh/N2G94G46**

# The Four Questions Answered

In the first section of this book I mentioned that there are four questions we need to ask of any moral theory. They spell the acronym **DARM** (**D**erivation, **A**pplication, **R**ealism, **M**otivation).

## 1. HOW IS THE IDEA OF GOODNESS DERIVED?

Goodness has to come from somewhere - it is, after all a human construct. The normal candidates are three:

1. God

2. Reason

3. Observation or experience.

**RELATIVISTS** argue that our idea of goodness comes directly from **CULTURE** (what JL Mackie in Inventing Right and Wrong calls "forms of life") or from **EXPERIENCE** (the utilitarian or situationist view that we judge right and wrong according to circumstances and likely consequences).

**NATURAL LAW** theorists like **AQUINAS** argue that goodness is partly an **A PRIORI** idea given by God - what he calls synderesis "the intuitive knowledge of first principles," and partly an **A POSTERIORI** idea worked out by experience as we develop our conscience and practical wisdom by looking at circumstances . Natural Law goods are in the end **OBSERVABLE GOODS**. We apply the **PRIMARY PRECEPTS** (acronym **POWER**) to situations.

**KANT** argues that morality is an **A PRIORI** category of the mind like number or cause and effect. Just as we need a concept of **NUMBERS** before we can count, so we need a concept of the **CATEGORICAL IMPERATIVE** before we can apply it to the world and synthetic experience where we discover how it works. Morality is therefore **A PRIORI SYNTHETIC**.

**UTLITARIANS** see goodness as a **TELEOLOGICAL** idea depending on the end we pursue, either **PLEASURE** (the psychological "sovereign two masters, pleasure and pain" of Bentham) or **HAPPINESS** (it is good because most people desire it as an end in itself, says **MILL**). So goodness is measurable, an **OBJECTIVE, EMPIRICAL IDEA**, either by counting **HEDONS** (Bentham) or **DESIRES** (Mill). This is therefore a theory appealing to **A POSTERIORI** knowledge because we cannot know consequences without some experience of them.

**DIVINE COMMAND THEORISTS** argue that God has revealed the moral law to us in **SCRIPTURE** which has commands like the ten commandments which we need to understand and then obey. We have an **INNATE** conscience, as St Paul argues we all (believer or non-believer) have "the law written on our hearts" (Romans 2:15). This implies **A PRIORI** God-given knowledge of good and evil.

Notice that only two of these theories are purely **DEONTOLOGICAL**, Kantian ethics and Divine Command Theory. **NATURAL LAW** has deontological outcomes (the **SECONDARY PRECEPTS**) which come from a **TELEOLOGICAL WORLDVIEW** because in Natural Law everything has a proper rational purpose (**TELOS**).

# 2. HOW ARE THE THEORIES APPLIED?

**RELATIVISTS** see goodness as relative to culture or experience and so any situation needs to be applied to the relevant cultural value. These may still be very **REASONABLE** but, argues the relativist, even **REASON** is culturally conditioned and not **PURE** as Kant implied.

**NATURAL LAW THEORY** applies the five primary precepts (acronym **POWER**) to produce the secondary precepts. So the **P** of **POWER** (preservation of life) yields the **SECONDARY PRECEPT** do not abort, do not commit suicide, do not murder. These are not **ABSOLUTE RULES** as we allow killing in time of war. Ultimately the primary precepts are derived from a socially relative idea of **HUMAN FLOURISHING** - what it means for a human being to live well or excellently.

**KANT** sees right and wrong as something irrational, a **CONTRADICTION** or logical inconsistency. There are two types of self contradiction: the **CONTRADICTION IN NATURE** includes suicide and breaking your promises. These cannot be willed universally without contradiction because **EUTHANASIA** if universalised leads to mass suicide of those in pain, and breaking your promise if universalised leads to the elimination of the idea of promising altogether. A **CONTRADICTION IN WILL** is not illogical, but cannot be universally willed or desired. We could never desire not to help our neighbour in distress because we would always want to be helped when we are in distress.

**UTILITARIANS** see the right action as one that maximises happiness or pleasure. So we need to examine the likely consequences, count how many are affected by our choice, and then apply the Greatest Happiness Principle. We apply utilitarian principles **CONSEQUENTIALLY**.

However, Utilitarians still have the challenge of explaining why I should have a **DUTY** to consider the interests or happiness of others (even complete strangers) in my utilitarian calculation. Can utilitarian ethics escape from this essential **EGOISM** and partiality - that my happiness or possibly mine and my family's has greater weight than the **GENERAL** happiness. Is **SINGER**'s universal objective viewpoint which assesses perferences of all affected by my action really possible or even desirable?

**DIVINE COMMAND THEORISTS** argue that we should obey God's commands because God is good. He is the source of goodness (holiness, perfection) and love (to a Christian this means **AGAPE** love or sacrificial love for the stranger). So anything he wills and commands must be good. We should not question God: just find a Bible verse that is relevant and apply it.

# 3. REALISM

How realistic are these theories from the perspective of modern sciences such as **PSYCHOLOGY** and **BIOLOGY**?

**RELATIVISM** fits well the postmodern world where there is no one overarching narrative accepted as true. It also fits **FREUDIAN** psychology where conscience comes from our upbringing and the sense of shame engendered by our parents and teachers. In the postmodern age we are taught to **TOLERATE** difference.

**NATURAL LAW** is often condemned as outdated. However the idea of a shared rational nature is something evolutionary biologists accept. **RICHARD DAWKINS** (The Selfish Gene) talks of a "lust to be nice" coming from our evolved sense of obligation to one another. Is this so different from **AQUINAS'** synderesis principle that we by nature "do good and avoid evil?" Dawkins rejects the **TELEOLOGICAL** nature of Natural Law, as there is no purpose to **EVOLUTION**, he argues, just an endless struggle to survive. But we have inherited an **ALTRUISTIC GENE** from this battle of the genes giving us a shared moral nature. The selfish gene is the self-promoting gene, but for humans, it is in our interest to be moral and so, argues Dawkins, the selfish gene gives us our moral sense and desire to help others.

**KANT**'s ethical theory can be criticised for being **DUALISTIC**. So he sees the world of experience, the **PHENOMENAL** world as opposed to the world of ideas, the **NOUMENAL** world. He also contrasts **REASON** and **EMOTION** in a way that seems to deny moral worth to an action done out of compassion rather than duty alone. The outcome of his theory, that categorical rules are **ABSOLUTE** can also be criticised as unrealistic. In practice we do lie to save someone's life - the goodness is situational, not absolute as Kant suggests.

**DIVINE COMMAND THEORY** suggests I can read God's commands from a Holy Book and then apply them easily to the present day. But this is unrealistic. The Bible says nothing about abortion, euthanasia, just war principles, or genetic engineering. So we have to interpret and extrapolate. What exactly did Paul mean by "women should keep silent in church?" (1 Corinthians 14:33) If we reject parts of Leviticus as no longer applying (stoning the adulterer for example) then what about other parts of the Bible? How do we decide? How should we extrapolate (extend) the principle "thou shalt not kill?" (Exodus 20:13) This seems to include a prior question - who or what has an absolute right to life (embryo, foetus, person on life support machine, soldier in war, civilian in war etc)?

# 4. MOTIVATION: WHY BE MORAL?

So we come to the final, and perhaps most pressing question. Why be moral at all? Why not live a life of selfish egoism and be a parasite on the goodness of everyone else?

**RELATIVISM** is a wide and ambiguous concept. Joseph Fletcher (Situation Ethics) defined himself as a relativist (Situation Ethics is a form of **CHRISTIAN** relativism). He argued that we are moral out of love for fellow human beings. But this begs the question why I should bother about fellow human beings when it's not in my interest to do so. Fletcher's answer was that we need to convert to the way of love - commitment comes before action. He calls this **THEOLOGICAL POSITIVISM**. Situation ethics is something of a special case and is arguably not a pure form of relativism as it has one **ABSOLUTE** at its centre - agape love.

**NATURAL LAW** theorists argue from a **TELEOLOGICAL** standpoint. Be moral, they say, because it is reasonable to want to flourish as a human being - to be the most excellent person you can be. A knife should cut well, says Aristotle, and a human being should be rational in order to flourish well. **AQUINAS** argues that our greatest happiness will be found by aligning the natural law with God's eternal law. This will cause us to be a full, complete human being.

**KANT** takes the stern, dutiful line of obedience to the moral law or **CATEGORICAL IMPERATIVE**. He argues that rational people will freely choose this way as the most logically consistent way of arriving at the **SUMMUM BONUM**, the greatest good. Autonomous human beings will realise that to obey the categorical imperative out of duty is the best way of building the best of all conceivable moral worlds. Like Kant himself, this moral law within should fill us with awe. It's wonderful. The summum bonum is a mixture of virtue (dutifulness) and happiness ultimately only discovered in heaven (Kant's postulate of **IMMORTALITY**).

**UTILITARIANS** are not agreed on what motivates us. **BENTHAM** thought we were psychological **HEDONISTS** motivated by the prospect of pleasure and avoiding pain. **MILL** disagreed. He thought pleasure and happiness were not the same, as happiness needed clear goals and strenuous activities. Happiness is to be found in challenges met and difficulties overcome - which sometimes can involve discipline and sacrifice. Why bother with the happiness of others? Mill answered, out of **SYMPATHY** for my fellow human beings. "In the Golden Rule of Jesus of Nazareth ('do to others as you would have them do to you,' Matthew 7:18), wrote Mill, "is all the ethics of utility."

**DIVINE COMMAND THEORY** argues for two motivations - love of God and fear of God. We should love God because he created us and first loved us and redeemed us by his Son. And we should fear him because he is holy and just and will one day judge us, as the **PARABLE OF THE SHEEP AND GOATS** suggests, according to how we have treated the poor, needy, homeless and vulnerable. "As you have done to the least of these, you have also done to me," says Jesus. Failure to love and obey God, if the same parable is believed will result in "eternal punishment," not "eternal life" (Matthew 25:45,46).

# Exam Rescue Remedy

1. Build your own scaffolding which represents the logic of the theory. Use a mind map or a summary sheet.

2. Do an analysis of past questions by theme as well as by year. Try writing your own Philosophy of Religion paper based on what hasn't come up recently.

3. Examine examiners' reports for clues as to how to answer a question well.

4. Use the **AREA** approach suggested in this revision guide. **ARGUMENT**- Have I explained the argument (from Plato or Kant for example)? **RESPONSE** - Have I outlined and explained a good range of responses to the argument? **EVALUATION** - Now I have clearly set out positions, what do I think of these? Is mine **A PHILOSOPHICAL** argument and why? Does the original argument stand or fall against the criticisms raised? Why or why not?

5. List relevant technical vocabulary for inclusion in essay (eg efficient cause, form of the good, analytic, synthetic).

6. Prepare key quotes from selected key authors, original/contemporary. Learn some.

7. Contrast and then evaluate different views/theories/authors as some questions ask "which approach is best?" So contrast every approach with one other and decide beforehand what you think.

8. Practise writing for 35 minutes. Don't use a computer, unless you do so in the exam.

9. Always answer and discuss the exact question in front of you, never learn a "model answer." Use your own examples (newspapers, films, documentaries, real life). Be prepared to think creatively and adapt your knowledge to the question.

10. Conclude with your view, justify it (give reasons) especially with "discuss."

# Appendix - Unit 2 - Area C

In this appendix you will find sections on **ABORTION**, **EUTHANASIA** and **GENETIC ENGINEERING**. These are popular issues that might be chosen for Unit 2 study.

# Abortion

## SOME DEFINITIONS

**ABORTION** can be natural (miscarriage) or by medical procedure (using drugs or killing and dismembering a foetus). A **FOETUS** exists from eight weeks onwards, when the embryo assumes the basic shape of the newborn and all the organs are present; an **EMBRYO** from conception to eight weeks. **PRE-EMBRYO** is now being used to denote the collection of cells up to 14 days old, before the **PRIMITIVE STREAK** emerges.

## LEGAL POSITION (UK)

The **1967 ABORTION ACT** legalised abortion up to 28 weeks with two doctor's consent: for medical reasons; for psychological reasons; for family reasons; in cases of disability. The legal term was changed in 1990 to 24 weeks. The age of **VIABILITY** has now dropped to 22 weeks with medical advances. 85% of abortions occur under 18 weeks and there are around 200,000 abortions a year in the UK, representing 25% of pregnancies. Note: we do not have "abortion on demand" in the UK as the consent of two doctors is needed.

# SANCTITY OF LIFE

**SANCTITY OF LIFE** (sacredness) - biblical view **GENESIS 1:27**, we are made in the image of God, and "he knit you together in your mother's womb," **PSALM 139:6**. Human life has **INTRINSIC VALUE** because God himself "became flesh and lived among us" (**JOHN 1:14**). We are not our own, but we belong to God and our life is "on loan" from God. God appoints the day of our death "the Lord gave and the Lord takes away" **JOB 1:21**. "Do not murder" is a fundamental law, **EXODUS 20:13**, implying respect for all human life, and to the Catholic Church this includes embryonic life.

**SANCTITY OF LIFE** - the Natural Law view. **EVANGELIUM VITAE** (1995 Papal encyclical) argues society has undermined sanctity of life and produced a "culture of death" in its attitude to foetal life, the elderly and the handicapped. So "every person open to truth can recognise the sacred value of human life from its beginning to its end" - as Paul notes "even Gentiles have the law written on their hearts," **ROMANS 2:14-15**. Abortion breaks two **PRIMARY PRECEPTS** of reproduction and preservation of life - as human life begins at conception. We know this through the **SYNDERESIS** principle: innately we "do good and avoid evil" in line with our rational purposes given by our human nature.

**SANCTITY OF LIFE** - weak view. Some prefer the more universal, weaker idea of **RESPECT** for life. As medical science advances we know more eg about disabilities of foetuses or inherited diseases. **SITUATION ETHICS** sees **AGAPE** as a universal good, so the person's situation needs to be paramount, and **STANLEY HAUERWAS** argues that the Church has permitted the taking of life in the past eg when it is in the interests of others, or in cases of martyrdom.

## QUALITY OF LIFE

Peter Singer maintains we would always choose a healthy child over a handicapped one. So "if aborting the abnormal foetus can be followed by having a normal one, it would be wrong not to do this." Note the usual consequentialist problem: how do we know? There is also the question of resources: how much does the handicapped child cost over its life relative to the healthy one? A utilitarian might argue the resources are better spent elsewhere. Is it the most loving outcome (Situation Ethics) to bring a suffering child into the world? Singer employs the **REPLACEMENT** argument - it is always better to replace a less happy child by a happier one - but does this justify **INFANTICIDE** - the killing of less healthy children? Or (as used to happen in Britain in the days of your family doctor) the smothering of abnormal infants?

## HUMAN RIGHTS

Some argue that because the foetus shares the attributes of a person it should have full human rights (including the right to life). The logic of the argument from human rights is given below (P = proposition).

- **P1** - The unborn child is a human life (Is it? Even as a collection of cells?).

- **P2** - It is always wrong to take innocent human life.

- **P3** - Abortion involves the taking of innocent life.

- **P4** - Therefore abortion is wrong.

Notice that the meaning of "human life" has changed from "biological life" to something close to "personhood." The meaning has changed from P1 to P2 - note also the addition of the moral word "innocent."

# WOMEN'S RIGHTS

**JUDITH JARVIS THOMPSON** employs the analogy of the violinist - after his friends kidnap you, you wake up plugged into a sick violinist who needs your kidneys. To unplug the violinist will kill him. It's only for nine months. Do you have the **RIGHT** to unplug the violinist? Does your right to choose what to do with your body outweigh the right to life? (Note the problems with this analogy - for example, pregnant women are not immobile, they are not kidnapped but choose to have sex, the foetus is arguably not actually a person). Thompson argues that to be forced to remain with a dependent being attached to you is **OUTRAGEOUS**.

# PERSONHOOD

**MARY ANNE WARREN** asks "what characteristics make a person?" She lists: consciousness, reason, self-motivated activity, communication, self-awareness. "Genetic humanity is not enough" - we must have at least one of these criteria. "A foetus is a human being which is not yet a person, so cannot have full moral rights," argues Mary Anne Warren. Note: if you apply her criteria this would allow you to kill infants, coma victims and people asleep! **SINGER** agrees with **TOOLEY** who declared a human being "possesses a serious right to life only if it possesses the concept of a self as a continuing **SUBJECT OF EXPERIENCES** and other mental states, and believes that it is itself such a continuing entity." Infants do not qualify. In 1979 **SINGER** wrote, "Human babies are not born self-aware, or capable of grasping that they exist over time. They are not **PERSONS**," therefore, "the life of a newborn is of less value than the life of a pig, a dog, or a chimpanzee."

# WHEN DOES LIFE BEGIN?

**CASTI CONNUBI** (Papal encyclical) - persons at conception. **RC CATECHISM** "from the first moment of his existence a human being must be recognized as having the rights of a person - among which is the inviolable right of every innocent being to life." The **PRIMITIVE STREAK** is the first recognisable feature at 15 days. **QUICKENING** (movement) occurs at 100 days (c 14 weeks). Some time between 18 and 24 weeks foetus feels pain. **VIABLILTY** (survivability out of the womb) exists around 22 weeks - but probability of survival is low. **MARY ANNE WARREN** sees birth as only morally relevant point as "the extension of equal moral status to foetuses threatens women's most basic rights. Unlike foetuses, women are already persons." **JONATHAN GLOVER** argues it is a matter of degree - a foetus is more of a person than an embryo, a baby is more than a foetus. Ultimately this is a **METAPHYSICAL** question to do with beliefs rather than science. **DON MARQUIS** argued that abortion is wrong because it deprives someone of a future and "the ethics of killing is self-evident" (but how do we know the future? What of the mother's future? How do we weigh mother against child?).

# CHRISTIANS AND ABORTION

There is not one Christian view. The conservative view held by many Catholics and evangelicals holds that life is sacred from the point of conception because God the creator is behind and within this creation (Psalm 139 "God knit you together in your mother's womb"). Catholics follow a **NATURAL LAW** argument, pointing to the **PRIMARY PRECEPT** of preserving innocent life, and the **DIVINE LAW** "do not murder," whereas evangelicals appeal only to **SCRIPTURE**, a Divine Command Theory, eg **PSALM 139:6** "God knit you together in your mother's womb." Liberal Christians might take a **SITUATION ETHICS** view of abortion, arguing that **AGAPE** (sacrificial) love is best maximised by considering the **PERSON** (but which person? mother? child?) and **OUTCOMES** (but how do we know?). Questions of **PERSONHOOD** are logically prior to any other judgement.

# UTILITARIANS

**UTILITARIANS** seek to do an empirical calculation of good over evil (or pleasure/pain). **HEDONIC** utilitarians like Bentham balance pleasure/pain (eg emotional, financial, personal pleasure/pain). **RULE** utilitarians (Mill) calculate from past experience what social rules maximise happiness (eg the misery/death caused by backstreet abortions vs happiness/misery of mothers having abortions). Rule utilitarians stress importance of **RIGHTS** and **JUSTICE**, but again, the question of whether the foetus is a person comes before we decide whether the mother's rights come before foetal rights. **PREFERENCE** utilitarians like **SINGER** might put more weight on a potential child's preferences, but in fact, Singer's view of personhood (rational self-consciousness) allows for **INFANTICIDE** of disabled children.

# KANT

Kant argues for rational, a priori **UNIVERSALISABILITY** of autonomous (free) human beings. Again, question of **PERSONHOOD** comes first, otherwise we might discount the foetus completely and only universalise the mother's autonomous (free, self-legislating) choice. The **FORMULA OF ENDS** states we should never use human beings as just a means to an end, but as an end in themselves - with dignity, rights, and autonomy of their own. Abortion seems to break this formulation - but only if the foetus is a person. If the foetus is just like an appendix, there is arguably no moral issue for a Kantian.

# GET MORE HELP

Get more help with abortion by using the links below:

http://i-pu.sh/G4C53F46

# Euthanasia

## DEFINITIONS

- **EUTHANASIA** (Greek = good death) - Is the practice of ending life to reduce pain and suffering (so "mercy killing").

- **VOLUNTARY** euthanasia - When a patient's death is caused by another person eg doctor with the **EXPLICIT CONSENT** of the patient. The patient request must be **VOLUNTARY** (acting without coercion, pressure) **ENDURING** (lasts some time or is repeated over time) and **COMPETENT** (they have the mental capacity to choose). A variation on euthanasia is **PHYSICIAN-ASSISTED SUICIDE** - this differs from euthanasia as the doctor will help the patient to commit suicide (eg set up the apparatus), but the final act of killing is done by the patient.

- **NON-VOLUNTARY** euthanasia - Is done **WITHOUT** the patient's consent, because they are not competent or able to give the consent (eg in a coma, on a life support machine). The doctor and/or the family may take the decision.

- **INVOLUNTARY** euthanasia - Is performed **AGAINST** the wishes of the patient. This is widely opposed and illegal in the UK.

## ACTIVE OR PASSIVE

**ACTIVE** euthanasia is the **DIRECT** and **DELIBERATE** killing of a patient.

**PASSIVE** euthanasia is when life-sustaining treatment is withdrawn or withheld.

This distinction may also be described as the difference between an **ACT** and an **OMISSION** (failing to act) and between **KILLING** and **ALLOWING TO DIE**. Some, such as James Rachels, argue there is no real difference - if anything passive euthanasia (withdrawal of treatment) is worse because it leads to a longer, drawn out death and so more suffering potentially. **DAME CICELY SAUNDERS** (who founded the hospice movement) argues that it is unnecessary for anyone to suffer a painful death with modern drugs. A counter-argument is that many doctors already hasten death (eg by doubling a morphine dose): under the doctrine of **DOUBLE EFFECT** if the intention is to alleviate pain and a secondary effect to kill someone, the doctor is not guilty of any crime.

## LEGAL POSITION

Until 1961 suicide was illegal in the UK. The **1961 SUICIDE ACT** legalised suicide but made it illegal to assist.

The **NETHERLANDS** and **SWITZERLAND** allow voluntary euthanasia (active and passive) and physician-assisted suicide. The **DIGNITAS** clinic in Switzerland helped 107 British people to die in 2010. **DR ANNE TURNER** (aged 66) was one such person in 2009 - subject of the docu-drama "A Short Stay in Switzerland." No-one has ever been prosecuted in the UK for helping a relative or friend go to Switzerland.

In 2010 Director of Public Prosecutions **KEIR STARMER** confirmed that relatives of people who kill themselves will not face prosecution as long as they do not maliciously encourage them and assist only a "clear settled and informed wish" to commit suicide. The move came after the Law Lords backed multiple sclerosis sufferer Debbie Purdy's call for a policy statement on whether people who help someone commit suicide should be prosecuted. In August 2012 Tony Nicklinson, with "locked-in syndrome," failed in his legal attempt to end his "intolerable life."

Keir Starmer concluded: "There are **NO GUARANTEES** against prosecution and it is my job to ensure that the most vulnerable people are protected while at the same time giving enough information to those people like Mrs Purdy who want to be able to make informed decisions about what actions they may choose to take."

The **OREGON RULES** are another attempt to legalise assisted suicide by laying down conditions under which it will be allowed in US law.

## SANCTITY OF LIFE: BIBLE

The Bible argues that life is a gift from God. Humans are created in the **IMAGE OF GOD** (Genesis 1:27) and the **INCARNATION** (God taking human form - John 1:14) shows the sacred value of human life. Human life is a **GIFT** or **LOAN** from God: "The Lord gave and the Lord has taken away," (Job 1:21). We should also show **RESPECT** for human life: "thou shalt not murder" (Exodus 20:13). We should also "choose life" (Deuteronomy 30). Finally, Christian love (**AGAPE**) is crucial (1 Corinthians 13 "the greatest value of all is love"). We should protect human life (the parable of the Good Samaritan) particularly as God gave his only son to redeem us (bring us back from sin and death) and give us the gift of "life in all its fullness."

# SANCTITY OF LIFE: NATURAL LAW

The **NATURAL LAW** view argues that there is a **PRIMARY PRECEPT** to "preserve life" and views life as an **INTRINSIC** good. Euthanasia is therefore wrong and the Catholic Church forbids both active and passive euthanasia as "contrary to the dignity of the human person and the respect due to God, his creator" (Catechism of the Roman Catholic Church). However, the **DOCTRINE OF DOUBLE EFFECT** might accept the shortening of human life (eg if the intention is to relieve pain, secondary effect to kill) so long as it is only a **FORESEEN BUT UNINTENDED RESULT**. The Catholic Church also makes a distinction between **ORDINARY** means (ordinary, usual medical treatments) and **EXTRAORDINARY** means (treatments that are dangerous, a huge burden, or disproportionate). It is morally acceptable to stop extraordinary means, as "it is the refusal of over-zealous treatment."

"Discontinuing medical procedures that are burdensome, dangerous, extraordinary, or disproportionate to the expected outcome can be legitimate; it is the refusal of "over-zealous" treatment. Here one does not will to cause death; one's inability to impede it is merely accepted. The decisions should be made by the patient if he is competent and able or, if not, by those legally entitled to act for the patient, whose reasonable will and legitimate interests must always be respected." Catechism 2278

# QUALITY OF LIFE

**JAMES RACHELS** argues that the sanctity of life tradition places too much value on human life and there are times (eg with abortion and euthanasia) when this is unhelpful. He makes a distinction between **BIOLOGICAL LIFE** ("being alive" = functioning biological organism) and **BIOGRAPHICAL LIFE** ("having a life" = everything that makes us who we are). He says that what matters is biographical life and if this is already over (for example in a **PERSISTENT VEGETATIVE STATE** - **PVS**), then taking away biological life is acceptable.

**PETER SINGER** argues that the worth of human life varies (the value of human life is not a sacred gift but depends on its **QUALITY**). A low quality of life (judged by the patient) can justify them taking their life or justify someone else doing it for them.

## AUTONOMY

**JOHN STUART MILL** (On Liberty, 1859) argues that individuals should have full **AUTONOMY** (the freedom to make decisions without coercion) so long as it does not harm other people. Individuals cannot be compelled to do things for their own good - "over his own mind-body the individual is sovereign." Those who support voluntary euthanasia believe that personal autonomy and self-determination (choosing what happens to you) are crucial. Any competent adult should be able to decide on the time and manner of their death.

**KANT** assumes autonomy as one of his three key postulates (with God and immortality). We are self-legislating, free moral beings. However, he argued in an essay on suicide that suicide was self-contradictory as, if it was universalised, the human race would die out.

# ARGUMENTS AGAINST EUTHANASIA

1.  **PALLIATIVE CARE** - Dame Cicely Saunders argues that there is a better alternative for euthanasia in providing a pain-free death for terminally ill patients. The **HOSPICE** movement may be seen as an alternative, but, the euthanasia supporter might argue, this level of care is not available to everyone, is expensive and cannot fully relieve a patient's suffering (eg for someone who cannot breathe unassisted).

2.  **VOLUNTARY AND COMPETENT** - some raise questions about voluntary euthanasia. Can the patient ever be free from coercion (eg relatives who want an inheritance or doctors who need to free up resources)? Is the patient likely to be competent (eg when under high doses of medication, or when depressed, or senile). Response would be that there are at least some clear cases when patients **ARE** clearly voluntary (not coerced) and competent. Guidelines such as Starmer's or the **OREGON RULES** require a certain time period of repeated requests to different people, which are then independently confirmed.

3.  **SLIPPERY SLOPE** - this is the argument that once allowed, the outcome will be a process of a further decline in respect for human life and will end with the practice of non-voluntary euthanasia for the elderly seen as "unaffordable" by the working majority. A response might be that there is a clear difference between voluntary and non-voluntary euthanasia. Is there any evidence of a slippery slope in the state of Oregon or Switzerland? The rules on assisted suicide are drawn up precisely to stop the slide into widespread disrespect for human life.

4.  **DOCTOR-PATIENT RELATIONSHIP** - some argue that doctors have a duty to preserve life (the **HIPPOCRATIC OATH**). Euthanasia will undermine the trust between patient and doctor

if there is a fear that they will seek to end their life. However, as with abortion, there will remain doctors opposed to euthanasia which a patient could always choose, and it is highly unlikely that GPs will have any say in the process of mercy killing.

## GET MORE HELP

Get more help with euthanasia by using the links below:

**http://i-pu.sh/S0L72D29**

# Genetic Engineering

Genetic Engineering (**GE**) involves the practice of changing the genetic makeup of plants, animals or humans, or taking recombinant **DNA** (hybrid **DNA** made by artificially joining pieces of DNA from different sources) and using it for a special purpose. Novel reproductive technologies, such as those used in the cloning of sheep like Dolly, do not technically involve **GE**. A **GENE** is a sequence of **DNA** made up of just four chemical letters. There are approximately 24,000 genes in the human body. If all the **DNA** in all the cells in one person were stretched out they would reach to the moon and back 8,000 times. 20% of our genes are now **PATENTED** by those who discovered them. Similarly **GM SEED** is owned by the seed company that engineered it - and cannot be sown without their permission (or purchase).

# ISSUES

1. For what **PURPOSE** (making money? choosing eye colour? eliminating disease?).

2. With what **CONSEQUENCES** for biodiversity (plants) or human flourishing (**EUDAIMONIA**)?

3. Who decides? Do we as parents have the **RIGHT TO A CHILD** who is disease free? Is this an individual or social issue?

4. Should we **PLAY GOD** and manipulate nature?

5. Will a **SLIPPERY SLOPE** develop where one change leads to further unanticipated bad effects - such as the lowering of value of those with disabilities?

# PRESENT POSITION

The **GENOME** was fully sequenced by Craig Ventner by 2003 . Now it is possible to screen for genetic defects (**PRENATAL GENETIC DIAGNOSIS - PGD**) as part of IVF treatment, alter genetic makeup **IN UTERO** (in the uterus) and create **GENE THERAPIES** from **STEM CELLS** for potential treatment of various diseases. **DOLLY** the sheep was cloned in 1996 and had three parent sheep - one provided the egg, one the DNA and one the womb (though the South Korean scientist who claimed to have cloned humans proved to be a fraud). **CROPS** have been genetically modified by companies like **MONSANTO**.

# THE LAW

The **HUMAN FERTILITY AND EMBRYOLOGY ACT** (2008) established an authority for regulating genetic engineering in humans (the **HFEA**). **CLONING** is illegal unless a special **LICENCE** is obtained (first granted in 2004). Human and animal gametes can also be mixed (**NEWCASTLE UNIVERSITY,** 2006). **GENETIC ENGINEERING** of embryos is allowed in order to prevent a disability/ genetically inherited disease. **MULTIPLE** embryos can be fertilised - with issues of embryo wastage as the **BEST** are selected (shades of the wise men of Sparta selecting which baby lived or died). Or sperm can be injected directly into one egg - which most Christians find perfectly morally acceptable as no **WASTAGE** of embryos occurs. In the UK you cannot **DESIGN** a baby except for medical reasons - to create **SAVIOUR SIBLINGS** as in the film **MY SISTER'S KEEPER**.

# UNNATURAL

Natural Law theory suggests we should not change the inviolable ousia (essence) or telos (goal) of any living organism. Both concepts come directly from Aristotelian philosophy. The GE of female turkeys to make them less broody (so that they lay more eggs), has been attacked by Jeremy **RIFKIN** as 'a serious violation of the intrinsic value of the creature'. RC Church argues that "a strictly therapeutic intervention whose explicit objective is the healing of various maladies such as those stemming from chromosomal defects will, in principle, be considered **DESIRABLE**, provided it is directed to the true promotion of the personal well-being of the individual without doing harm to his integrity or worsening his conditions of life." (Donum Vitae). But **CLONING** is absolutely prohibited, and embryo **WASTAGE** considered as evil as **ABORTION** - an assault on the **SANCTITY OF LIFE**.

## PLAYING GOD

Is GE good **STEWARDSHIP** or evil **DOMINION** (Genesis 1:26)? One-third of all agricultural production world-wide is lost to pests and diseases, and there is enormous scope for GE to render crops resistant to pests, drought and frost, to improve yields and to enable food to be produced in harsh environments. Some Christians argue we should use the new technology to feed a hungry world and to distribute its benefits more equitably. Others fear the consequences of upsetting biodiversity or exploiting poor farmers who are buying seed that they cannot re-sow next year. There is a evidence of a rise in suicide rates among Indian farmers who have been sold patented GM seed - is there a link?

## CONSEQUENCES

There are 5,000 inherited diseases which could be eliminated with mass genetic screening. Is this not a moral **GOOD**? Others argue that the **SANCTITY OF HUMAN LIFE** is violated and there will be **SOCIAL CONSEQUENCES** such as the change in perception about human suffering or the creation of a super-race (with two tiers of society like in the film **GATTACA**). To eliminate imperfections is to change the idea of being human, bowing to the **UTILITARIAN** argument that anything that produces human suffering is wrong, which many Christians reject due to the **REDEMPTIVE SUFFERING** of **JESUS** on the Cross.

## RIGHTS

Do I have the **RIGHT TO CHOOSE** the genetic makeup of a child? Or to have specially designed child to save another? Do I have a **DUTY** not to bring into the world a child who will suffer (perhaps in the same way as I did as a person with a genetic disease?) Does a child have the **RIGHT**

**TO KNOW** who are their genetic parents? Since 2005 the answer is "yes" - and sperm donor fathers have declined rapidly. Who has the right over a **SURROGATE** baby? Suppose the mother changes her mind? In America a famous case, the case of **BABY M**, involved a surrogate mother who changed her mind and refused to hand the baby over. The Catholic Church approves **GENETIC THERAPY** but disapproves strongly of **GENETIC ENHANCEMENT** where a child's characteristics are improved.

The production of human beings selected according to sex or other predetermined qualities, which change the genotype of the individual and of the human species, are contrary to the **PERSONAL DIGNITY** of the human being, to his integrity and to his identity. Therefore they can be in no way justified on the pretext that they will produce some beneficial results for humanity." Donum Vitae, Roman Catholic encyclical

Many people argue that GE opens a new era of **EUGENICS** so discredited by Nazi ideology, where genetic breeding is used to create a super-race.

## KANT

Kant's second formulation of the Categorical Imperative, the **PRINCIPLE OF ENDS** states that humans should never be treated just as a **MEANS** to an end but always an **END** in themselves. Designer babies and genetic enhancement seem to violate this principle. But what of **EMBRYO WASTAGE**?

It's not clear Kant would ever have accorded a collection of cells (whose gender etc was indeterminate) the **AUTONOMY** necessary to be human. If I knew I was going to be born with a genetic defect, would I choose to be born - applying **UNIVERSALISABILITY**? It seems clear that a **RATIONAL** human would choose to be born without a genetic disease.

Perhaps the Kantian answer continues to depend on the status we accord the **PRE-EMBRYO** (what doctors are starting to call an embryo up to 14 days old before the **PRIMITIVE STREAK** emerges).

## GET MORE HELP

Get more help with genetic engineering by using the links below:

http://i-pu.sh/S3N01V81

Lightning Source UK Ltd.
Milton Keynes UK
UKOW04f2115280314

229042UK00001B/6/P